Original title:
In the Arms of Forever

Copyright © 2024 Creative Arts Management OÜ
All rights reserved.

Author: Charles Young
ISBN HARDBACK: 978-9908-0-0938-4
ISBN PAPERBACK: 978-9908-0-0939-1

The Sway of Time in Our Embrace

Tick tock, the clock won't stop,
We dance like penguins, slipping, plop!
With every twirl, a giggle breaks,
As we stumble, our laughter shakes.

Eons might pass, who really cares?
We'll trip on dreams, forget our pairs.
Gravity laughs, it pulls us low,
But we'll twirl faster, steal the show.

Hearts Bound by Eternal Light.

Like fireflies caught in sleepy nets,
We buzz around with silly bets.
Eternity's got nothing on us,
Cheesy jokes, our favorite fuss.

You say I'm weird, I call it charm,
In our madness, there's no alarm.
Infinity grins, it cannot fight,
With a wink and a nudge, we shine bright.

Eternal Embrace

We hug like bears who've lost the plot,
In a tangle of limbs and a hot, hot pot.
Forever's a word that's lost its way,
In every burp and stylish sway.

Time has joined the silly spree,
Stumbling about, it can't quite see.
With hugs so tight, we bound and weave,
In this tangled bliss, we'll never leave.

Whispers of Timelessness

Our whispers dance like bubbles in air,
Floating around with exquisite flair.
Every shared joke, a spark so bright,
We'll laugh through the day, and into the night.

Old age may knock, but we won't mind,
We'll tease and frolic, forever aligned.
In the mess of life, just you and me,
A comedy show, don't you agree?

Boundless Love's Shelter

When you steal my fries at noon,
I roll my eyes, but it's a tune.
You laugh and say it's love's delight,
As we share bites, all feels just right.

Your quirky socks, they clash in hue,
But add a flair that's oh so new.
We dance in mismatched, joyful glee,
In our own world, just you and me.

Together Through Endless Days

The laundry pile, a mountain high,
We tackle it with goofy sighs.
Your dance moves in the living room,
Turn chores to jokes, and bust the gloom.

We'll binge on shows and eat some cake,
Laugh at the choices that we make.
With every cuddle, every tease,
You're my best friend, and that's a breeze.

In the Grip of Eternity

Your snoring's like a soothing song,
I'm up all night, it won't be long.
Yet in that chaos, warmth I find,
You're so absurd, and oh so kind.

Each morning coffee's a new chance,
To laugh at life, our little dance.
From silly jokes to puddle splashes,
Time ticks slow while laughter clashes.

A Haven Beyond Time

Your glasses misplaced, on your head,
You sigh and say you're half brain-dead.
Yet in this chaos, love does bloom,
As we create our joyful room.

We're partners in the greatest scheme,
Chasing dreams like a wacky team.
With every hiccup, every fall,
Our laughter echoes, that's the call.

Echoes of an Ageless Heart

I danced with a sock on my head,
We laughed as we fell on the bed.
Time ticked away like a silly old clock,
Life is a joke, and I'm just the punchline of the talk.

Tickle wars stretch on 'til the dawn,
Chasing the sun while wearing a fawn.
Each wrinkle a laugh line, a badge of the past,
In a world full of giggles, we're having a blast.

The cat joins the party, all fuzzy and bright,
He's plotting a heist on our food for tonight.
With each silly moment, we craft our own song,
These echoes of joy will forever last long.

Chasing Infinite Horizons

We raced on our bikes down the old grassy hill,
The wind in our hair gave us all of the thrill.
With maps made of crayons, we plotted a quest,
To find the best ice cream, where flavors expressed.

The horizon seems endless, like my snack stash at home,
Each mile brings more laughter, no reason to moan.
We stumbled and giggled, made mud pies so grand,
In this endless adventure, together we stand.

With lakes full of frogs and trees to climb high,
We're co-pilots of chaos, just you and I.
Charting a course for the wildest of dreams,
As the stars wink at us, we'll follow their beams.

The Ties That Bind Forever

With shoelaces tangled, we tripped over fate,
Laughing so hard, our sides felt like great.
Each secret we shared, a goofball delight,
Building our fortress in the glow of moonlight.

Through pranks and odd outfits, we crafted our lore,
A tapestry woven with silly rapport.
If life is a rodeo, let's ride it with glee,
Two clowns in the circus, just you and me.

From toast to burnt lunches, we savor it all,
In this kitchen of chaos, we take the fall.
With a wink and a nudge, we find our sweet way,
These ties that we share will never decay.

Twilight of the Evermore

As shadows grow long, we build silly forts,
Throwing pillows and laughs, in our make-believe courts.
With fairy lights twinkling, we dance in the gloom,
Creating our stories inside this small room.

The clock strikes a note as we sip fizzy drinks,
In this twilight of laughter, no need for the blinks.
Each goofy grin shared is a treasure we find,
In the pages of a story that time left behind.

With bedtime adventures and monsters we chase,
In our dreamland of giggles, we've carved out a space.
Through twilight's embrace, we'll never be bored,
In this realm of pure joy, we've truly adored.

A Mosaic of Timeless Moments

In a world of puzzling quirks,
We dance like awkward birds.
Your socks will never match,
Yet, love shows in silly words.

We trip on love's own toes,
And laugh at every fall.
Like clowns in a grand parade,
You're my favorite punchline, after all!

With each absurd misstep,
We scribble laughter's tune.
In this silly waltz of ours,
We spin 'neath the grinning moon.

So let's wear those mismatched shoes,
And chase the day's delight.
In our collage of giggles,
Everything feels just right.

Anchored in Endless Affection

You bring the punch to my boredom,
With puns like sea-salt spray.
Your jokes are my life's anchor,
In a tide of disarray.

Our love's a rubber lifeboat,
Bouncing on stormy seas.
Like pirates seeking treasure,
The map is drawn in cheese!

Your laughter's my compass rose,
Leading to shores of glee.
Even when the winds are wild,
Together we sail carefree.

In this ocean of nonsense,
We navigate with flair.
Each wave of mirth a reminder,
How much fun it is to care!

The Tapestry of Eternal Embrace

You're the thread in my fabric,
Stitched with odd little quirks.
Like a cat in a wool sweater,
We tangle with playful smirks.

Each day we weave our story,
With laughs and little falls.
Patterns of chaos and joy,
Call it love with no walls.

In a patchwork of moments,
We patch holes in our hearts.
Every stitch tells a joke,
And laughter never departs.

So let's pull on the yarn,
And create something grand.
A masterpiece of mischief,
Crafted right by our hands.

Hidden in Infinite Shadows

In the shadows where we play,
Whispers of laughter bloom.
Like shadows dancing lively,
Life's a slightly silly room.

We lurk behind the curtains,
As mischief takes its flight.
With every prank we pull,
The world feels warm and bright.

From sneaky hidden giggles,
To whispers, soft and sweet.
Each chuckle paints a picture,
Of shadows in retreat.

Together in this twilight,
We hide and seek with glee.
In the world of sweet shenanigans,
You're my favorite mystery.

A Dance Beyond Time

In a shop of mismatched socks,
Two lost souls found their clocks.
They tangoed past the laundry pile,
With every spin, a goofy smile.

A waltz through cereal boxes galore,
Dodging spills and sticky floors.
They laughed as the time did slip away,
In this dance, forever's here to stay.

Chasing shadows of silly dreams,
On this stage, nothing's as it seems.
Gliding through life like a soap bubble,
Bumping into joy, what a delightful trouble!

So here they whirl, those quirky two,
In dance shoes of mismatched hue.
No end in sight, they spin around,
In love's embrace, forever found.

Celestial Bonds

Once two stars in a tangled mess,
Bumped into each other, oh what a guess!
They giggled in cosmic, silly delight,
Waltzing through galaxies, shining bright.

One flared like a disco ball,
The other just tripped and had a fall.
They spun through space with wild abandon,
Creating supernovas like a star-studded band on.

In the universe's funny plot twist,
Who knew they couldn't resist?
As comets crashed with splashes of glee,
They declared, "We are meant to be!"

So here they play in the night sky,
Chasing beams of light, oh my!
In the laughter of space, they declare a pact,
A bond more fun than any love abstract.

Enchanted by Timeless Love

In a garden where time goes haywire,
Two playful hearts spark a fire.
They chased butterflies through a maze,
Lost in giggles, in a magical daze.

They pranced on tulips as tall as they stood,
Wishing on dandelions, just like they could.
With wands made of licorice and dreams,
Every moment bursting at the seams.

They painted the skies in candy hues,
Dancing away their silly blues.
With a wink and a nod, they twirled and spun,
In a love that's frolicky, oh what fun!

So when they whisper 'timeless' at dusk,
It's wrapped in sweetness and a hint of musk.
In their kingdom of laughs and carefree sighs,
Forever's found in giggles and highs.

The Fortress of Endless Affection

In a castle made of jellybeans,
Two jesters built their love scenes.
With a moat of chocolate, they made their stand,
Life's sweet battles fought hand in hand.

They skipped on walls of marshmallow fluff,
Together they laughed, never enough.
With rubber chickens as their swords,
They conquered the world with playful chords.

In the banquet hall of silly delights,
They dined on cake in whimsical nights.
Arm in arm with giggles a-swing,
Creating a future that makes joy sing.

So in this fortress of laughter so bold,
Their story of love forever retold.
For in every chuckle, in every embrace,
They built a stronghold where silliness had its place.

Timeless Hearts Intertwined

Two hearts do the tango, a silly dance,
Where leg cramps meet love, oh what a chance!
With each clumsy step, a giggle breaks free,
'Tis a comical sight, just you and me.

The clock spins around, but we lose track of time,
Counting giggles and snorts, our own little rhyme.
As laughter fills spaces that silence won't dare,
We build a fortress of joy, floating in air.

Side by side we sit, with popcorn to share,
Munching on dreams like we've not a care.
A ticklish embrace, where time starts to bend,
Every tickle and tease, we always commend.

As days turn to years, a riddle unfolds,
Our quirky adventures are treasures to hold.
With mismatched socks and a love note in hand,
We're the jesters of life, in our whimsical land.

A Voyage Through Unending

Set sail on a sea of melted ice cream,
Navigating flavors, living the dream.
With sharks made of jelly and waves of delight,
We'll giggle through storms, into the night.

Our ship may be wobbly, but who's keeping score?
With candy bar sails, who could ask for more?
Charting a course through the clouds of sweet bliss,
Kissing fluffy clouds, a sugary miss.

Oh, captain my captain, do you feel the breeze?
It's wafting with whispers of cotton candy trees.
We'll dance with sea turtles, in laughter, we'll dive,
In this voyage of giggles, we'll always survive.

As we reach the shore of the land made of dreams,
We'll feast on the humor that life often screams.
Every wave is a joke, every tide is a cheer,
Together we sail, with nothing to fear.

The Garden of Infinite Dreams

In a garden where laughter grows free in the sun,
Blooming flowers of giggles, oh what a pun!
Each petal a joke, each stem a delight,
We'll frolic and tumble, from morning to night.

The daisies all dance, the tulips they tease,
Sunflowers nodding, as if they agree.
With honeybee chuckles buzzing nearby,
We'll twirl with the daisies, oh me, oh my!

In this quirky green haven, where dreams come alive,
We'll play hopscotch with daisies and jive through the hive.
Frogs dressed in tuxedos serenade in a rhyme,
In our garden of joy, we'll savor sweet time.

As the stars twinkle down on our leafy cocoon,
We'll sip lemonade laughter, beneath the full moon.
Forever, my friend, this garden will glow,
With the joy of remembrance for all we will sow.

Love's Eternal Canvas

With brushes of laughter, we paint our sweet fate,
Coloring moments, never too late.
Splashes of joy flicker bright in the air,
Creating our masterpiece, beyond compare.

Each stroke tells a story, a giggle unfolds,
With swirls of bright orange and stripes of bold golds.
We scribble our names in a sky full of bliss,
A canvas of love sealed with a silly kiss.

Oh, the palette of life, with its ups and its downs,
We'll laugh through the chaos, compose silly sounds.
Like a connoisseur's joke, we sip on the fun,
From this canvas of heart, we're never outrun.

As time plays its tricks, and the colors may fade,
Our cartoonish creation will never be swayed.
For in laughter and love, our brush strokes align,
Creating the artwork of joy that is divine.

The Path to Unending Love

We danced on clouds of cotton candy,
With giggles that made the stars feel dandy.
Your winks are sweets, a sugar high,
Together we laugh as the hours go by.

Chasing our dreams on roller skates,
Mismatched socks and crazy plates.
We trip on love, it's quite the race,
Yet, in this journey, we find our place.

Kites made of laughter soar so high,
With pizza parties beneath the sky.
Never a dull day with you around,
Life's a circus, and we're the clowns!

So here's to us, with silly charms,
Forever young in each other's arms.
Our hearts collide in a playful dance,
Let's keep this joyful, wild romance!

Forever's Silent Vow

Your silly face when you eat ice cream,
Makes me giggle, like a daydream.
We share secrets in cookie crumbs,
A quirky bond that overcomes.

We snap our fingers to a funny tune,
Under the watch of the laughing moon.
In a world of chaos, we stay so bright,
With silly jokes that light up the night.

When socks go missing, we start a quest,
To find the rogue ones, we're truly blessed.
A treasure hunt on our living room floor,
Can you hear our laughter? It's never a bore!

As we sip our soda, in goofy style,
Life's a fun ride, let's stretch each mile.
With silent vows and playful grins,
In this wacky life, love always wins!

The Enchantment of Endless Days

In a land where dreams jump and play,
We'll make today always feel like May.
With rainbow hats and polka-dot shoes,
Every moment's a chance to choose.

We'll build a fort with pillows galore,
And giggle as we pretend to snore.
A kingdom of laughter, where joy will reign,
With you by my side, there's no room for pain.

Magic beans to grow a beanbag chair,
We'll drift through the air without a care.
Floating on giggles, we'll surf the breeze,
Chasing sunsets with the greatest ease.

So let's keep wandering through this delight,
With candy dreams glowing soft in the night.
For in our hearts, a spell is cast,
In this enchanted world, we'll forever last!

Whispers in an Infinite Sea

In the ocean of giggles, we make the waves,
A splashy duet of silliness saves.
We ride the tide of silly chatter,
In this vast sea, laughter's the platter.

Mermaids dance with shoes made of foam,
As we build a castle, our quirky home.
Seagulls echo our laughter loud,
Together we shine, oh how we're proud!

With every wave comes a ticklish breeze,
A concoction of fun that aims to please.
We'll dive beneath with grins so wide,
In this endless sea, love is our guide.

So let the whispers of joy be clear,
As we ride together without any fear.
In our aquatic realm, where giggles roam,
We've found our place, the best kind of home!

Forever's Gentle Hold

You tripped, I laughed, we fell in a heap,
Your sandwich flew, it's now in the deep.
We rolled on the grass, just too much to bear,
Your face was so funny, with bread in your hair.

In moments like these, time seems to freeze,
The clock doesn't tick, it just takes a tease.
You pinched my cheek, I splashed you with tea,
Forever's a joke, come chuckle with me.

We dance in the rain, your socks are all wet,
We won't care at all, no reason to fret.
With giggles as currency, smiles all around,
In this silly world, joy is profoundly found.

So take my hand, let's leap into fun,
With laughter our guide, oh, the things we've begun!
Forever's not serious, it's marked by our play,
In every wild moment, we'll just seize the day.

Embraced by the Infinite

You told me a joke, and I snorted my drink,
The laughter exploded, what a funny link!
With each silly story, our spirits take flight,
A friendship so bright, it's a pure source of light.

We dance like two ducks, flapping with glee,
You stole my last fry, oh, the audacity!
Yet here we are, laughing, pretending it's fine,
In this wacky adventure, you're always divine.

Through hiccups and giggles, we stumble and sway,
You always find ways to brighten my day.
Time simply chuckles, as it rushes on by,
In our joyous chaos, even seconds seem shy.

So let's spin around, as the stars start to wink,
With a tickle and nudge, let's not stop to think.
In a hug of the cosmos, we revel and play,
Together forever, in our own funny way.

A Symphony of Timeless Affection

Your socks don't match, but who even cares?
With laughter and quirks, we're the perfect pair.
We hum a strange tune, offbeat yet bright,
In a busker's delight, we're artists at night.

Each glance is a giggle, each hug has a joke,
Our humor's a potion, it surely invoked.
We dance with the ketchup, we twirl with the fries,
In this kitchen ballet, each moment just flies.

You told me I'm weird, I just raised an eye,
Is that really true? Oh no, not I!
In our playful banter, the world's just a stage,
We'll script our own comedy, no need for a cage.

So let's share our dreams, with bubbles and cheer,
In this symphonic mess, you're the one I hold dear.
With timeless affection, we'll sing loud and clear,
In a chorus of laughter, we'll write our own sphere.

Whispers of an Endless Bond

I spilled my drink, and you shook your head,
Yet laughter erupted, as we sat on the bed.
Your giggle's a whisper, my heart skips a beat,
In the chaos of life, you make it all sweet.

We plot our pranks, like a duo of glee,
With rubber chickens and wild fantasies.
As the sun starts to set, we plot our next spree,
In a world that's so funny, it's just you and me.

Every inside joke's a thread in our quilt,
A tapestry woven with all the joy built.
We chase after chuckles, we live for the fun,
Two stars in the sky, just laughing as one.

So let's spin our tales, with nonsense and smiles,
We'll dance through the ages, traverse cosmic miles.
In whispers of joy, with a wink and a bond,
We'll cherish forever, of this we respond.

A Love That Defies the Clock

Time ticks on like a silly clock,
Yet together we dance, two left feet in a flock.
With mismatched socks and hair out of place,
We giggle and stumble in our own little space.

Days might be numbered, but we don't have dread,
For each tick is a blessing, not a reason to spread.
We binge-watch the moments like it's our last show,
Laughter our currency, in rich overflow.

Wrinkles will find us, of that, I am sure,
But with your silly grin, I can only endure.
Let's toast to the chaos, and the time we borrow,
Each awkward misstep paints a joyful tomorrow.

So let the hours fly and the minutes take wing,
In this madcap affair, love is our zing.
A love beyond calendars, or clocks with a chime,
With you, dear companion, I could bumble through time.

Paths Intertwined Through Infinity

Our paths, like spaghetti, all tangled in knots,
Yet somehow we wander to the silliest spots.
With your hand in mine, we'll get lost in the crowd,
Two quirky explorers, distinct and yet loud.

Infinity's vast, like a buffet of dreams,
With flavors of joy, and giggles in streams.
We'll munch on our memories, a delectable choice,
As we sing off-key, with endless rejoice.

In a world full of puzzles, we'll solve with a laugh,
Crafting our future from the silly half.
Together we'll trip over love's silly trails,
Creating a saga where goofiness prevails.

So here's to our journey, forever misfit pair,
Navigating life with a jig and a flair.
In these intertwined paths, humor will reign,
For love is the punchline, and joy is the gain.

Glimpses of Forever in Your Eyes

When I look in your eyes, I see some quirks,
A glimmer of mischief and slightly wild smirks.
Those moments we share, with a wink and a grin,
In the jests of our lives, that's where love begins.

You trip as you dance, and I can't help but chuckle,
Each slip and each fall is another sweet snuggle.
We giggle through storms and play in the sun,
Our forever is funny, we always have fun.

In a game of charades, you're a card shark of grace,
Yet I'm the comedian, none can take my place.
You roll your eyes, but I know you adore,
This wacky love tale that we both can explore.

So here's to the laughter, the paths that we choose,
Where each glance is a mirror of thrills we can't lose.
In your twinkling eyes, oh how time flies high,
Each chuckle's a promise, as bright as the sky.

Revelations of Timeless Togetherness

You and I, a duo of delightful oddity,
In this timeless tale, we embrace the sodality.
We'll wear silly hats while sharing our cake,
With icing on noses, what a cute mistake!

Moments stretch on like a stretchy old sock,
Each day's a new episode—watch our love rock!
With pranks and sweet giggles, we'll craft our today,
Chasing down sunsets, come what may.

Your laugh is my soundtrack, my favorite refrain,
Living in silliness, joy pouring like rain.
We'll frolic through jungles of candy and cheer,
Hand in hand wandering, there's nothing to fear.

So here's to forever, as goofy as grace,
In laughter we flourish, finding joy in each place.
With no need for a map or a clock set to chime,
Together, my darling, we'll bask in our prime.

When Hearts Dance Beyond Time

When we twirl like two left feet,
Laughter echoes, oh so sweet.
Chasing time with silly glee,
Who knew love could be this free?

Tick-tock goes the silly clock,
Wearing mismatched socks on the block.
We trip and fall, then rise again,
Dancing like fools, oh where's the pain?

With twinkling eyes, we skip and play,
Making memories day by day.
In this dance, we lose all care,
Forever young, a joyful pair.

So here's to us, the goofy kind,
Time flies, but we don't mind.
With every laugh, we steal the show,
In this rhythm, we forever flow.

The Infinite Embrace of Us

You stole my fries, I stole your heart,
In this game, we both play the part.
Sharing secrets through cheesy grins,
Love's a battle, but where's the sins?

With goofy faces, we strike a pose,
You nibble my ear while striking a rose.
Tickle me pink, you make me sigh,
In this funny world, we'll always fly.

On a pizza date, we spill some sauce,
Each delight's a comical loss.
You hold my hand as we both chide,
Our quirks unite, we won't abide.

In the chaos, we find our groove,
Two silly souls in a perfect move.
With every chuckle, we twist and twirl,
This dance of love, oh what a whirl!

Shadows of Eternity Cast by Light

Cast in shadows, we laugh and play,
Invisible threads lead us astray.
Dancing under the moon's bright glow,
Who needs a map when we go with flow?

With silly hats and giant shoes,
We roam the night, we cannot lose.
Conversations that go off the rails,
Our love story told in goofy tales.

When shadows grow long and dreams take flight,
We giggle and tease, oh what a sight!
In this fun fair, we'll never part,
Forever young, you know my heart.

In every flicker, every little spark,
We find our joy; we light the dark.
Hand in hand, carving our path,
In this love, we find the math.

Tides of Forever at Our Feet

As waves crash down, we splash and squeal,
In our silly world, it's a big deal.
With sand on noses and sun on cheeks,
We chase each other through sunny peaks.

The ocean's song is a silly tune,
We dance like mermen under the moon.
With plastic shovels and buckets wide,
In this moment, we take pride.

While seagulls squawk at our shrieking joy,
You're my treasure, my merry buoy.
Through tidal pools, we laugh and roll,
Forever may we soak in this soul.

So let the waves carry us on,
Each silly tide brings a brand new dawn.
In laughter's grip, we find our seat,
In this ocean, life feels so sweet.

Love's Endless Horizon

On a beach we both did play,
Building castles through the day.
You said, "Look! A seagull flies!"
I replied, "With noisy cries!"

Our laughter echoed through the air,
Chasing waves without a care.
You took a dip, and I just watched,
Then found my clothes were all botched!

With sandy toes, we danced around,
Your goofy moves drew quite a crowd.
A crab joined in, he showed his skills,
Now he's our friend, and eats our meals!

So let the tides roll, let them sway,
We'll make memories every day.
Like silly kids, we'll chase the sun,
In this wild love, we've really won!

Cradle of Forever Moments

In the kitchen, we prepare a feast,
Pasta's twirled, you take a chance, at least!
Your sauce splatters on the wall,
Turns out dinner was a food fight after all!

We laughed so hard, we dropped the bread,
The cat now thinks our thoughts are fed.
He licked the floor, joined in our mess,
What a fancy little gourmet fest!

As we clean up, you try to pout,
I tickle you, and here comes the shout!
Also the dog wants to join the fun,
Can't say my love, we're quite the run!

Through the chaos, love's laughter blooms,
Our kitchen's filled with funny tunes.
This life we live, oh what a ride,
With all the snacks, you're by my side!

Where Time Surrendered

The clock ticks loud, but we dance slow,
Under twinkling lights, we put on a show.
You stepped on toes and sang off beat,
Yet still somehow, it feels so sweet!

The neighbors peek through windows wide,
Shaking heads, but they can't hide.
With every spin, you twirl and fall,
We laugh so hard, they join the call!

A sock flies high, a snack goes down,
Dancing like fools in our little town.
Turns out time bends when joy is near,
So let's just laugh and shed a tear!

In this moment, we'll never part,
With every giggle, you own my heart.
So here we stay, in this joyful dance,
Caught up in life's silly romance!

The Infinite Within Us

You've got a joke that makes me snort,
You told it wrong, but that's your forte!
We giggle through the night, don't need a court,
For love's just silly, in its grand ballet!

With ice cream sundaes, we make a mess,
A cherry lands straight on your nose!
Laughter bubbles, pure happiness,
You're a clumsy clown, I suppose!

Our heartbeats hum like a funky tune,
Every glance, a spark flies up to the moon.
Two oddballs making the best of fate,
With hugs and kicks, we seal our state!

As moments blend, the world fades out,
In this blissful chaos, there's no doubt.
With each silly giggle, we learn to trust,
Forever feels better, just being us!

Embrace of Endless Time

With socks that don't quite match, we stroll,
Laughing at the laundry's wild control.
A dance with dust bunnies in the hall,
In our quirky world, we have a ball.

The cat thinks he's the king of the chair,
We take turns, but it's not really fair.
We share popcorn in a movie fright,
Giggling as shadows jump in the night.

In silly hats, we'll wander the streets,
With ice cream cones and goofy feats.
The tickle of time wrapped up in jest,
In this messy life, we are truly blessed.

Whispered Promises Under Starlight

Beneath the stars, we make a toast,
To midnight snacks we love the most.
With cookies crumbled on the floor,
We laugh 'til our stomachs can't take more.

You stole my fries, I stole your drink,
In this playful mess, we hardly think.
A whisper sweet as whipped cream delight,
We plan our prank wars deep into the night.

The moon winks at our silly charade,
With creaky swings, our laughter cascades.
For promises made with giggles and grins,
In this cosmic joke, love always wins.

Boundless Horizons of Love

We dream of skies in polka dot hues,
With jellybeans raining down as our muse.
Kites tangled in hair and free spirits high,
Together we'll soar, really, oh my!

Let's chase the sunset in mismatched shoes,
With our playlist of very old tunes.
Every adventure, a comedic ride,
In a love story that we both abide.

Our hearts beat to the rhythm of fun,
Chasing shadows as we laugh and run.
With every step, laughter fills the air,
In this boundless world, life's beyond compare.

The Unbroken Thread of Tomorrow

We knit our dreams with yarn of light,
Every stitch pulls us close, feels just right.
With coffee spills on our favorite chair,
We stumble through life without a care.

Pajama days turn into a spree,
In belly laughs, we find harmony.
So here's to our future, wild and bold,
Wrapped tight in tales, endlessly told.

With silly selfies and dance-offs in sight,
Our hearts twirl beneath the soft moonlight.
For tomorrow awaits, bright and sublime,
With humor as glue, we conquer time.

The Unwritten Chapters of Us

In a world that loves to tease,
We scribble notes on falling leaves.
Each glance a plot twist, bold and bright,
In our funny, love-filled flight.

We dance like socks that lost their match,
Each giggle, another quirky patch.
The unwritten tales of me and you,
Are laughter blooms in morning dew.

Our story's page is dog-eared now,
Spelling love in a happy row.
Filled with pranks and playful dreams,
Writing life in vibrant beams.

So here's to chapters yet to come,
With funny quirks that make us hum.
Together we'll pen our sweet delight,
As the pages turn into the night.

Cradle of Endless Dreams

In a cradle spun from silly schemes,
We toss our wishes like moonbeams.
Each snort and chuckle lights the sky,
Turning yawns into cheerful sighs.

We sail on clouds of cotton candy,
Tickle fights and dreams so dandy.
With every laugh, our spirits soar,
In this kingdom where fun's hardcore.

Our pillow forts are castles grand,
As we dance circa a rock 'n' band.
In this cradle, laughter's the key,
Unlocking joy for you and me.

So come, my dear, let's dream anew,
With funny tales that ring so true.
In this laughter-filled scenario,
We'll always find our way to glow.

Journey Through the Infinite

Our journey starts at bizarre bends,
With maps drawn in crayon, let's pretend.
We'll take the path where giggles lead,
And plant our love like joyful seeds.

We'll ride on puddles, skip on rain,
Chasing clouds that look like planes.
In this quest we'll lose our shoes,
Follow the trail of happy clues.

Our roadmap is made of whimsy's thread,
Every stop is where we've laughed and bled.
With silly faces and silly grins,
This journey has no losses, only wins.

So come along, my playful friend,
Through fields of giggles, never end.
With every step, our hearts will sing,
In this infinite joy that life can bring.

Where Love's Light Never Fades

In this place where silly smiles thrive,
Our love's the spark that keeps us alive.
With each quirky joke, we light the way,
Chasing shadows that try to stay.

We frolic where the laugh lines trace,
In every hug, a warm embrace.
The moments we seize in playful glee,
Are lights that twinkle, just you and me.

With silly songs and dance reprieves,
We weave a tapestry no one believes.
In this realm where friendships bloom,
Love's light bursts forth, igniting the room.

So here's to us, forever fun,
With laughter bright like a morning sun.
In this garden where joy cascades,
Our love remains, and never fades.

Eternal Echoes of Our Bond

We dance like socks on polished floors,
Chasing echoes beyond closed doors.
Laughter spills like soda pop,
In this silly game, we'll never stop.

Your jokes are puns that make me cringe,
Yet every giggle feels like a binge.
Like cats on noodles, we twist and twirl,
In the chaos, I find my world.

With each misstep in this waltz we make,
You're the punchline of my every break.
Together we're a hilarious sight,
Under the stars, we shine so bright.

Love's Unfading Horizon

We chase the sun like ants on a hill,
With sandwiches packed, we have our fill.
Your cheerfulness wraps like a warm sweater,
In our goofy sketches, we're even better.

The horizon giggles at our silly ways,
With mismatched socks, we embrace the craze.
Like two peas in a pod, we're cooking up fun,
In our jestful realm, we've already won.

Every sunbeam whispers a joyful jest,
In our playful lives, we are truly blessed.
Around us, laughter dances and sways,
In this domain, we find our best plays.

A Canvas of Infinite Moments

We paint our days with colors so bright,
Every brushstroke brings pure delight.
Your smudged smile adds a whimsical splash,
In this masterpiece, our hearts are bold and brash.

Every tick of the clock is a giggling sound,
On this canvas, we'll always be found.
Fingers dipped in paint, we create our glee,
Each moment is art, just you and me.

With every tickle and every shared grin,
In this playful life, we always win.
Together we sketch our lives with flair,
A gallery of chuckles hanging in the air.

Timeless Caress in Twilight

The twilight kisses us with a wink,
As we ponder things that make us think.
Like fireflies dancing in the cool night,
Our giddy hearts take flight with delight.

With every giggle, we find a way,
To transform night like it's a play.
Your voice, a melody wrapped in cheer,
Makes the ordinary feel quite dear.

As shadows stretch and stars emerge,
We ride this wave, let laughter surge.
In this timeless space, we find our zest,
In the twilight glow, we are truly blessed.

The Glow of Timeless Affection

In a world where socks do roam,
A lost one finds its way back home.
We giggle at the tales we weave,
Like witty jokes that never leave.

Your laughter bounces off the walls,
Like rubber balls in echoing halls.
We dance like penguins in a zoo,
With makeshift moves, just me and you.

The clock may tick, the years may fly,
Yet here we are with glimmering eye.
A bond that's forged with silly fights,
Like jesters under moonlit nights.

In each chaos, there's delight,
With every shared, outrageous sight.
Eternity feels like a joyful jest,
With you, my dear, I feel so blessed.

Infinite Love's Haven

In our cozy nook of daily grind,
You steal my fries, but I don't mind.
With chocolate sauce and popcorn fluff,
Who knew that love could taste so tough?

We joke about our wrinkles claimed,
As laughter's echoes keep us framed.
Your quirky dance is quite bizarre,
Yet silly moves just raise the bar.

Endless tales echo through the hall,
Of epic fails, but we stand tall.
You snort when you laugh, I can't resist,
In this sweet haven, we coexist.

Like shoes misplaced or keys that flee,
We tackle life so carelessly.
In this absurdity, I find my glee,
Together forever—just you and me.

Threads Woven Through Time

We stitch our lives with laughter bold,
Like mismatched socks and stories told.
Your quirky quirks are priceless gems,
Like secret codes between old friends.

With each slip, we find our grace,
Your goofy grin lights up the space.
Crafting memories through playful stunts,
In the tapestry of life, we're the front.

Threads that tangle but never break,
No matter what, it's love we make.
From noodle fights to pancake art,
You hold the map right in my heart.

Through years that dance and times that lean,
In this collection, we build a scene.
Together we weave our joyful rhyme,
Forever friends for all of time.

The Depths of Togetherness

In a sea of mismatched schemes,
We float on laughter, chase our dreams.
Your snickering fits make my day bright,
In our little boat, we navigate light.

With cereal spills and coffee stains,
You make mundane feel like champagne.
Our jokes are treasures, each one unique,
A shared giggle always feels antique.

We stumble through life with hearts so wide,
Building a ship from silly pride.
With every wave, we find our song,
In goofy rhythms, we both belong.

Through the whirl of chaos and bliss,
Moments of madness become pure bliss.
In this ocean, we sail astound,
Together, my love, we gladly drown.

Moments That Stretch Into Infinity

We laughed till the sun turned bright,
Chasing shadows, what a sight!
With cupcakes stuck in our hair,
Life's silly twists are beyond compare.

Our cat thinks she's a dog, it's true,
Chasing squirrels like she has a clue.
Fetching sticks? Oh, what a show!
Life's little moments steal the glow.

We dance like nobody's watching us,
Twirl and trip, it's all a fuss.
Dinner's burnt, but who really cares?
Laugh it off as we part our hairs.

Through puddles, we splash and glide,
With goofy grins, our worries slide.
Time may bend and stretch away,
But joy is here, come what may.

The Pulse of Timeless Love

My heart races with a honk and a beep,
Love bloats like dough, in circles we leap.
Overcooked pasta on dates we roam,
But still, you're my favorite loopy poem.

Coffee spills as we gift a wink,
Caught in love, we hardly think.
Life's a rollercoaster, strap in tight,
Riding the waves of pure delight.

Juggling chores takes the prize,
I toss the socks; you roll your eyes.
Chasing silly dreams, we dive,
These sweet moments keep us alive.

With books that pile up like clouds,
We escape the world, laughing loud.
Timeless quirks, like mismatched socks,
In our fortress of love, we unlock.

Unraveled Threads of Forever

We knit life's chaos, a funky quilt,
With mismatched patterns, love is built.
Socks that disappear, where do they go?
They party unseen, just like our flow.

In awkward dances, we stomp and sway,
Feet tangled up in a freaky ballet.
Out of rhythm, but who needs a beat?
Our life's a circus, oh, what a feat!

Cereal for dinner feels so right,
Your face in the fridge became my light.
Sharing secrets over popcorn fights,
Finding joy in our wild delights.

Through tangled threads and silly threads,
A love that outshines our shared misreads.
We stitch each laugh and stitch each tear,
A patchwork of moments, a bold love affair.

Serenity Beneath the Eternal Sky

Peanut butter sandwiches on a starry night,
Counting constellations, a curious sight.
Spilled juice on the blanket, oh what a mess,
Yet laughter wraps us, like a warm caress.

We chase fireflies with fumbled feet,
Dodging the grass ticks, a funny feat.
Under the stars, we blurt out dreams,
Wishing to catch each giggle that beams.

Clouds drift by, like jellybeans,
Frolicking shadows dance in routines.
A serenade sung by the evening breeze,
Helium balloons float with such ease.

Here's to the moments that softly sigh,
With each glance up at the endless sky.
Beneath this vastness, we find our place,
In a world of laughter, we embrace.

The Light of Infinite Togetherness

In a world that's often crazy,
We find joy, oh so hazy.
With socks that never seem to match,
Together we create our patch.

Laughter spills like lemonade,
In this dance under the shade.
Our puns might make the neighbors frown,
But we wear jokes like a crown.

Each mishap makes us grin wide,
A twirl, a slip, a silly ride.
With every laugh, we hit replay,
In our fun-filled cabaret.

As the sun melts into the sea,
Your laugh will always comfort me.
In our bubble, we'll not stray,
In our antics, we'll forever play.

Sheltered by the Everlasting

Underneath the quirky stars,
We build dreams with chocolate bars.
Silly secrets we do share,
Like who forgot to comb their hair.

With blanket forts that touch the sky,
And popcorn battles, oh my my!
Our giggles echo through the night,
In this odd little delight.

We tell tales of our wild pets,
And make up silly little bets.
Who can balance on one shoe?
The wildest feats we both will do.

In a world so vast and grand,
Together we will always stand.
Joy and laughter as our guide,
Two goofy souls, side by side.

Embracing the Never-ending

A dance of quirks, a mishap spree,
Cereal for dinner, just you and me.
Swapping dreams and silly grins,
Where every loss just feels like wins.

With rubber chickens on the floor,
We find joy in every chore.
Dancing chaotically in place,
Wearing smiles, that's our grace.

Each moment feels like a splash,
With you is always such a bash.
Trying new things, like toe-tackling,
In our hearts, the laughter wrackling.

So here's to dreams that never fade,
And funny jokes we've always made.
Together we're a comedy,
In this grand fun-filled odyssey.

The Warmth of Eternal Nights

Under the glow of neon lights,
We feast on ice cream, endless bites.
With silly hats and funny faces,
In this world, we find our places.

Swaying to music only we hear,
Making memories that bring us cheer.
With each snack and silly dance,
We stumble into our own romance.

The moon winks at our funny ways,
We laugh 'til dawn in a wondrous haze.
With goofy selfies as our guide,
We embrace this joy, arms open wide.

As stars flicker in the dark sky,
Together we can always fly.
Through every giggle, every hug,
Life's funniest moments, warm and snug.

Symphony of Endless Tomorrow

In the garden of dreams, we play,
Where weeds dance and flowers sway.
We serenade the sun so bright,
While squirrels join in, what a sight!

Time ticks slower with a wink,
We debate if pink is for the sink.
Every moment a funny twist,
In this silly, wondrous mist!

With laughter as our guiding star,
We prance around like goofballs, ha-ha!
Our hearts compose a happy tune,
Beneath the glow of a laughing moon!

So here's to a dance that never ends,
Where silly math makes all the bends.
Tomorrow's symphony starts anew,
With a tickle and a laugh from you!

The Lasting Touch of Love

A gentle poke, a playful shove,
Your eyes twinkle, oh, what a love!
We chase each other 'round the halls,
Dodging laundry piles that fall!

You steal my fries, I'll take your socks,
We build our fortress out of blocks.
With every giggle, our bond grows tight,
Who knew love could be so light?

In this playful game we play,
Who's the winner? No one can say!
With crumbs in our hair, we nap and dream,
The best kind of love is bursting at the seam.

A tickle here, a nudge when needed,
Each touch, a laugh, our joy is seeded.
Forever feels like just a day,
In your company, I'd choose to stay!

Woven Into the Fabric of Time

Like mismatched socks on laundry day,
We laugh at time, it goes our way.
Each moment stitched with threads of cheer,
In fabric soft, our joy is near.

We weave our tales with mismatched twine,
Creating patterns divine, oh so fine!
With puns and giggles that never fade,
In this quilt of ours, we've truly played!

The clock may tick, but we ignore,
With ice cream sundaes, who could ask for more?
Every thread a memory, rich and bold,
In our tapestry, our love unfolds.

So come my dear, let's stitch some more,
With every laugh, we'll explore.
In this timeless fabric, we reside,
Woven tightly, side by side!

Horizons Painted with Eternal Strokes

We splash the sky with colors bright,
Cracking jokes in morning light.
Like canvas artists, wild and free,
Painting mishaps, just you and me!

With brushes dipped in laughter's hue,
We craft a world with shades anew.
Every sunrise, a joke unfolds,
Horizons bold with stories told!

In this gallery of silly dreams,
We mix our paints, oh how it gleams!
With every stroke, we find our way,
A masterpiece created in our play.

So grab that brush, let's make it fun,
With colors of love, we'll never be done!
In these horizons, we find our spark,
As we dance with joy from dawn till dark!

The Bridge to Timelessness

I once saw a bridge made of cheese,
But it crumbled with a little squeeze.
We laughed as it melted away,
Like our worries on a sunny day.

With each step, my socks did slip,
On a banana peel, I took a dip!
You cackled loud, I couldn't catch,
A moment that we surely matched.

The birds above quacked with delight,
Wishing us joy in our silly flight.
We danced on clouds, so bright and rude,
Creating laughter, a silly mood.

So here we are, hand in hand,
A journey that's just like a band.
With peanut butter and jelly dreams,
We'll float forever, or so it seems.

Horizons of Unfading Love

On a ship made of toast, we set sail,
With a crew of ducks, how could we fail?
Seagulls squawked, stealing our bread,
But we just laughed at the crumbs we shed.

The sun painted gold on our silly hats,
As we rode the waves on rubber spats.
Each wave a chuckle, every splash a grin,
We painted our hearts with silly whim.

With jellybeans as stars in the sky,
We wished for rainbows, oh my, oh my!
A treasure map that squiggled and swirled,
Led us to giggles around the world.

And as we danced on candy hearts' floor,
Chuckles spilled out as we begged for more,
Forever's a joke that we can play,
In the songs that laughter will always sway.

The Comfort of Eternal Whispers

In a garden where sunflowers grin,
We whispered secrets to the wind.
Bees buzzed with their drilly tunes,
While squirrels juggled acorns like buffoons.

A koala danced on a pogo stick,
Telling jokes that made us giggle quick.
With silly hats, we pranced and spun,
In our world, each day was fun.

The leaves chimed in with a rustling cheer,
As we guffawed till the stars appeared.
Moonlight tickled the clouds above,
In our twilight, we found our love.

So here's to whispers that never fade,
In the laughter we lovingly made.
With each chuckle, time can't bind,
A comfort in silliness of every kind.

A Journey into Infinity

On a rollercoaster, we twirled and flipped,
Each twist a giggle, each turn a trip.
With marshmallow clouds beneath our feet,
We soared through the air, oh what a feat!

Chocolate rivers in the sky so vast,
We dipped our toes in memories past.
Holding hands while rollerblading on air,
Spinning in circles, without a care.

A leprechaun popped out for a chat,
Wearing a tutu and a big old hat.
He claimed his luck was stuck at the door,
But we laughed it off, wanting more.

With each silly moment, we chased the sun,
In this zany ride, we had our fun.
An infinity shaped by laughter's song,
In a world where we always belong.

Infinity's Gentle Touch

Time flies by with silly grace,
As we chase our worries in this race.
A bubble bath with rubber ducks,
In a world of smiles, we're just plain lucks.

With every giggle, we defy the clock,
Dancing like penguins, it's quite the shock.
We whisper dreams on puffy clouds,
In a harmony of laughter, we sing out loud.

When life gets tricky, we play the fool,
Like juggling chickens, it's our golden rule.
Through every folly, love runs deep,
In silly dances, our secrets we keep.

So here we stand, with goofy hearts,
Crafting joy as life imparts.
In this moment, eternity we find,
With a wink and a grin, we leave the grind.

The Lasting Dream

Dreams are silly, like a cat on a train,
Chasing its tail in a playful gain.
Through every nap, we leap and play,
In the land of giggles, we'll always stay.

With giant cupcakes and ice cream skies,
We dance with shadows that wear bright ties.
In this quirky world, let's take a chance,
On trampoline clouds, let's laugh and prance.

Caught in daydreams where wishes run wild,
You and I, forever like a child.
With socks on our hands, we build a parade,
In this laughter-filled realm, we'll never fade.

Every chuckle is a moment we keep,
In the tapestry of joy, we dive so deep.
So hold my hand, let's twirl through the scheme,
Together we weave the fabric of dream.

A Canvas of Endless Love

Colors splash like laughter on a wall,
As we paint our tales, we'll never fall.
With crayons of giggles and brushes of fun,
Our masterpiece shines, two hearts become one.

Each silly stroke tells stories untold,
In a gallery of smiles that never grow old.
With every doodle, our quirks entwined,
Creating a canvas where joy is defined.

We'll splash bright hues in the silliest ways,
Like wild Picasso in a playful daze.
In this endless picture of laughter and cheer,
We'll color the world, forever near.

So let's paint the night with a vibrant hue,
As we twirl through a field of stars and dew.
With each brush of love, our hearts visible,
On this canvas of wonder, we're invincible!

Threads of Forever Tied

Two silly socks, forever matched,
In a dance of chaos, we're hand-snatched.
With knots of laughter and frayed edges fine,
We thread our stories in the grand design.

From tangled yarns that tickle the toes,
To patchwork moments that nobody knows.
Through laughter's fabric, we sew the day,
In this quirky quilt, we'll always stay.

Like clowns at play, we twist and we turn,
In the vibrant threads of love, we learn.
With every stitch, a memory sewn,
In this tapestry of joy—we've grown.

So here's to mishaps and love so wide,
In the threads of life, forever tied.
With a wink and a chuckle, we'll never part,
For in this creation, you hold my heart.

Foreverly Yours

In a world where socks go missing,
A love that's never dull, not hissing.
You steal my fries, I steal your drink,
Together we make quite the link.

Your snoring's like a bear on a spree,
Yet I wouldn't trade you, just wait and see.
In our dance of chaos and glee,
It's you, my friend, who completes me.

Every joke, a pun, our laughter roars,
You drop your lunch, I'm on all fours.
A bond, so silly, it has no end,
My partner in crime, my sweetest friend.

With sticky notes left without a clue,
I write, "I love you" as you misplace your shoe.
A journey together, forever amusing,
With you by my side, there's no losing.

Emotions Without an End

You called me 'darling' while on the phone,
But tripped on a cat, and you fell like a stone.
I laugh till I cry, under midnight's glow,
Our love is ridiculous; it just flows.

In a world of giggles and silly hats,
You serenade me with songs of stray cats.
Each moment a treasure, a fun little spree,
With you I'm the best, just let it be.

No romantic dinners, just tacos and fries,
We dance in the kitchen; oh how time flies!
From coffee spills to epic cake fights,
Our love is a riot, full of delights.

Who needs diamonds? I'll take your laugh,
In this crazy life, you are my better half.
Emotions like jellybeans, all colors blend,
A never-ending laugh, my perfect friend.

The Light That Never Fades

You light up my world like an old bulb's glitch,
With moments of joy that make me twitch.
Our love's a cartoon, always on screen,
With antics so quirky, it's fit for a queen.

Remember the time we danced in the rain?
You slipped, did a twirl, but felt no pain.
Laughter echoing, we made quite a splash,
You dubbed it romance; I dubbed it a crash!

When we share snacks, it's a delightful crime,
We plot and plan while eating sublime.
A little chaos, a dollop of cheer,
In the light of our laughter, there's nothing to fear.

Though the world grows dimmer and dreams might fade,
With you, my compass, the laughs never trade.
The glow of our giggles forever stays bright,
Together forever, oh what a delight!

The Allure of Endless Possibility

With you, every day is a sitcom, it's true,
From pillow fights to eating fondue.
We craft funny tales, our stories unwind,
With laughter and joy, what treasure to find!

In a dance of quirks, we trip and we fall,
But from goofy missteps, we always stand tall.
Mismatched socks and a funny little dance,
A life full of mishaps, but oh what a chance!

We'll climb every mountain, through thick and through thin,
In a game of charades, you'll always win.
With jokes on repeat, and glee mixed with cheer,
The allure of us could last for a year.

So here's to the chaos, the laughter we share,
In this wild adventure, I know you'll be there.
With every new dawn, my heart skips a beat,
Together forever; oh, life is so sweet!

Beyond the Veil of Time

Time's a silly old clown,
Juggling moments that frown.
We dance on its unsteady beams,
Laughing at our wildest dreams.

Around the clock, we chase the fun,
While seconds skip, a race we've won.
Tick-tock plays a playful tune,
As we boogie 'neath the moon.

In this comical tripsy whirl,
Each tick is a wink, a twirl.
Giggling softly as we run,
Together, time is never done!

So when the hands begin to fold,
We laugh at tales too bold.
Beyond the veil of what we find,
It's just a jest, not too maligned.

Love's Everlasting Symphony

A symphony of chuckles bright,
In every note, we find delight.
With trumpet blows and flute's sweet sighs,
We dance like bugs in butterfly guise.

The cello grumbles, bass joins in,
Snicker notes make laughter spin.
In perfect tune, our hearts combine,
Each quip and giggle divine.

Harmony flows, absurd and grand,
We sway like weeds in a funky band.
As double basses stomp and boom,
Even silence joins to loom.

And when the curtain starts to fall,
We stand and cheer, we've had a ball.
For love's a joy, a funny rhyme,
An everlasting, silly chime.

Cradled by Cosmic Time

Stars giggle in a cosmic sway,
As planets spin in a silly play.
Meteor jokes zoom by our side,
While comets grin in joyful glide.

We float on clouds of cotton candy,
In a universe decidedly dandy.
Galaxies wink with radiant glee,
Cradled by fate, just you and me.

With each tick of cosmic watches,
We dance through space, oh how it botches!
Quasars sing and nebulae gleam,
This journey, oh what a whimsical dream!

Through black holes we'll swirl and spin,
Playing tag where time begins.
Together we'll canvas the celestial dome,
In our silly ether, we find our home.

Eternal Sunsets Together

Sunset hues, a giggling blaze,
Painting skies in silly ways.
Each evening's laugh, a grand display,
As daylight bids the stars to play.

With toast in hand, we cheer and grin,
For dusk's a party, let's begin!
Rays of orange tickle the night,
Every blink is pure delight.

As crickets chirp a playful song,
We sway to dusk where we belong.
Eternal joy in twilight's grip,
Sipping dreams on a twilight trip.

So as the sun dips down to stay,
We'll laugh through night till break of day.
An endless giggle, my friend so dear,
With every sunset, we find our cheer.

The Palette of Forever

With brushes dipped in joy and cheer,
We splash our laughter, far and near.
Colors blend in a vibrant swirl,
Where every giggle starts to twirl.

A canvas stretched from dawn to dusk,
With paint that smells of silly musk.
Each stroke we make, a twist of fate,
Like cats in hats who celebrate.

Under the sun, we dance and play,
Chasing our worries far away.
In a world so bright, we find it clear,
Forever's just another year!

So paint your dreams with shades of fun,
And let your heart outshine the sun.
For in this game of pure delight,
We'll color life both day and night.

Boundless Dreams Unfold

In realms where silly socks do roam,
And marshmallow clouds build you a home.
We stretch our dreams and bounce around,
On trampoline stars where joy is found.

With every leap, we touch the sky,
Where gummy bears and rainbows lie.
Our laughter echoes through space and time,
Like penguins rhyming in perfect mime.

So chase the stars on jelly beans,
With hopes tucked in our polka dot jeans.
In whimsy's grasp, we'll take a ride,
On candy boats with love as our guide.

And as we sail through skies so grand,
With cupcake sails and dreams so planned,
We'll find the treasure, sweet and bold,
In stories yet to be retold.

An Odyssey Through Infinity

On ships of cheese, we sail away,
With pirate hats that look like clay.
In oceans filled with fizzy drink,
We toast to dreams with pen and ink.

The compass spins, the map unfolds,
With tales of giggles yet untold.
We dance with whales in tutu dress,
As stars align, we feel the zest.

Each wave we ride, a silly cheer,
With jellyfish that lend an ear.
Through cosmic loops and time's embrace,
We find our rhythm, let laughter race.

So grab your hat, the journey's near,
With nacho wishes and happy cheer.
Forever's road is quite the ride,
Where joy and dreams are side by side.

The Warm Glow of Infinite Love

In blankets made of cookies warm,
We gather 'round, it's quite the swarm.
With stories shared and smiles aglow,
Our hearts beat fast in friendship's flow.

Through ups and downs, we laugh and play,
With marshmallow hugs that save the day.
A glow that sparkles like a light,
In every silly, joyful bite.

With every hug, we feel the spark,
As kittens dance in dreams so dark.
Together, we create our song,
In harmony where we belong.

So let the warmth of love surround,
In every heartbeat, joy is found.
With laughter bright, we craft our fate,
In a world where fun is never late.

www.ingramcontent.com/pod-product-compliance
Ingram Content Group UK Ltd.
Pitfield, Milton Keynes, MK11 3LW, UK
UKHW020100171224
452675UK00013B/1236